HIGH SCHOOL BASKETBALL IN FAYETTE COUNTY

Pictured are the coaches of the teams located within Fayette County at a district tournament draw, probably in the early 1960s. They are (from left to right) S. T. Roach of Dunbar, Charles Livisay of Douglass, Elmer "Baldy" Gilb of Henry Clay, Fred O'Brien of Lexington Catholic, Gene Huff of University High, Bob Abney of Bryan Station, and Ken Caudill of Lafayette. (Courtesy of Gene Huff.)

Front Cover: Bruce Davis (42) of University High puts up a shot against Powell County while Carl Eldridge (45) looks on during the 1964–1965 season. The two teams played each other twice that season, with University High taking the first meeting by a score of 85-69 while the return game ended in a rare tie, 64-64. (Courtesy of Gene Huff.)

Cover Background: The Athens team of 1953–1954 includes, from left to right, (first row) Tommy Johns, Howard Blakeman, Bob Baesler, David Brumagen, Bobby English, and Kelley Lawson; (second row) Scotty Baesler, J. B. Wingate, ? Lawson, Luther Stivers, Billy Brisbay, Billy Guilfoil, Louie Allison, and head coach Bob Abney. (Courtesy of Bob Baesler.)

Back Cover: Lexington Catholic represented Fayette County and the 11th Region in the 2008 Sweet Sixteen and reached the semifinal stage before bowing out to Holmes High School. (Courtesy of Kismet Photography.)

HIGH SCHOOL BASKETBALL IN FAYETTE COUNTY

Dave Redden

ARCADIA PUBLISHING

ISBN 978-0-7385-6736-5

Published by Arcadia Publishing
Charleston SC, Chicago IL, Portsmouth NH, San Francisco CA

Printed in the United States of America

Library of Congress Catalog Card Number: 2008928813

For all general information contact Arcadia Publishing at:
Telephone 843-853-2070
Fax 843-853-0044
E-mail sales@arcadiapublishing.com
For customer service and orders:
Toll-Free 1-888-313-2665

Visit us on the Internet at www.arcadiapublishing.com

CONTENTS

Acknowledgments 6

Foreword 7

Introduction 8

1. Before 1950 9
2. The 1950s 15
3. The 1960s 29
4. The 1970s 51
5. The 1980s 75
6. The 1990s 91
7. The 2000s 109
8. They Coached in Fayette County 121

ACKNOWLEDGMENTS

This being my first foray into publishing, I am more than indebted to my editor, Luke Cunningham. From Day One, it seems that we have been on the same page with this project, and he has been the impetus to keep me on track and focused.

Equally important to this book's existence is my wife, Tanya, a reference librarian whose dogged determination to hunt down those elusive newspaper reports and out-of-print books as reference material was invaluable to the project.

The inclusion of the foreword written by coach Joe B. Hall is an honor for me. Even though I am not American, I have learned enough about the sport of basketball to know how revered and respected Coach Hall is not only in Central Kentucky, but also throughout the commonwealth and the nation.

Many other individuals and schools have aided me in my search for photographs, clippings, statistics, and general information. If I miss anyone, I apologize in advance, but my thanks go out to Gene Huff, Bob Baesler, Scotty Baesler, Billy Guilfoil, Louis Stout, Marilyn Mitchell, Janie Cantrell, Cindy Brooks, Amber Tongate, Tom Grunwald, Lynda Short, Sabina Massey, the Blue Grass Baptist School, Brandon Salsman, and Russ Day.

A project such as this could not be put together without the cooperation of my family. My wife, Tanya, has already been mentioned, but she should also be admired for the way she has put up with my late nights working on the project and my trips to various establishments to gather information. My children, Scott and Cassie, have also had to put up with my authoring antics while this publication was in progress. I would also like to mention my older children, David and Coral, who do not reside in Lexington, Kentucky.

To all of you . . . thanks a million!

Tates Creek senior Vince Taylor was named to the All-American First Team in 1978. He was also named a member of the *Concensus Magazine* All-American Team, First Team All-State, First Team All-City, and UPI's Player of the Year. Taylor also created a new school record by scoring 52 points in the final home game of the season against Jessamine County. (Courtesy of Tates Creek High School.)

FOREWORD

Kentucky's passion for high school basketball is known the world over. While some of the finest players from the Bluegrass state go on to play college and even professional basketball, the limelight for most lasts only four years. But in that short time, history is often created and changed, legends are made, and the annals of high school athletics are written for both the Davids and the Goliaths. There are few places in the commonwealth where the sport is more celebrated than in Fayette County. The Lexington area is home to some of the state's largest high schools, but its smaller public and private schools are also known for churning out premier teams and top notch talent.

During the past 50 years, Fayette County high school athletics and basketball in particular has weathered storms of social change, race, the effects of school district consolidation, and the stressful juggling of yearly budgets. The county's survival and the success of area programs have made Lexington the beating heart of high school basketball in Kentucky. As such, it seems appropriate that the Kentucky High School Athletic Association (KHSAA) state tournament should be held in Lexington every year. Regarded as the most sought after experience and distinguished honor in Kentucky high school sports, teams across the state—from the hollows of Floyd County, to the bustling streets of Paducah—duke it out all season long for a chance of making it to the state tournament.

Nearly every year, at least one Fayette County school walks onto the hardwood floor of Rupp Arena. Representing a county that lives and breathes the sport, the sacred moments do not pass unappreciated by these players. Some will go on to play collegiate basketball at one of the state's numerous and esteemed universities, and a few may even have the honor of joining the ranks of those legendary players whose jerseys hang in the rafters above Rupp Arena. But for most, that game will be their shining moment, and what they give and leave there will be their legacy.

Within the pages of *High School Basketball in Fayette County*, author Dave Redden gives sports fans a look back at some of Fayette County's legendary basketball programs. Profiling the schools, coaches, and players who shaped the Bluegrass state's reputation for competitive basketball, Redden's collection of photographs and captions breaks down more than 50 years of the county's basketball heritage. The result is a nostalgic reminder for those who were a part of it, an education for those who weren't, and an entertaining read for basketball fans statewide.

—Joe B. Hall

INTRODUCTION

In Kentucky, basketball is king. It is revered like no other sport, except maybe horse racing for two minutes per year. Fayette County and Lexington are the center of the hotbed. The University of Kentucky is in Lexington, and its storied basketball program shows the rich history of the sport in Central Kentucky.

In the early days, schools not only played other schools, but also some club teams such as the YMCA and alumni teams. In 1917, the Kentucky High School Athletic Association (KHSAA) was formed to bring some semblance of structure to sports in general within the schools.

The first recorded state championship was played in 1916, with Henderson defeating Somerset 37-14. The first KHSAA-sponsored state championship was played in 1918 and was won by a strong Lexington High School team, who defeated Somerset 16-15. This would be the first of three consecutive state championships for Lexington High School and six overall for the school, which eventually became today's Henry Clay High School.

Six championships are indeed impressive, and Lexington/Henry Clay is not the only Fayette County school to have achieved the feat. Lafayette equaled the record with a championship in 2001 under coach Don Adkins, but it was the teams of the 1950s that blazed a trail for the Generals. Coached by Ralph Carlisle and led by players such as Billy Ray Lickert, Lafayette won the title three times that decade.

Speaking of coaches like Carlisle and Adkins, it would be remiss of me not to mention a few of the hardworking leaders of the hard court such as Bob Abney, Charles Livisay, Nick Wanchic, Elmer Gilb, S. T. Roach, Louis Stout, Nolan Barger, Jock Sutherland, Danny Haney, Gene Huff, Frank Watson, Maurice Jackson, and John Heber—the list is endless. Many of these coaches are pictured in this book, but some are not, and we cannot forget the impact they have had on many young men's lives.

For many years, the black population played within a league of its own. Under the auspices of the Kentucky Negro Athletic Association (KNAA), schools such as Lexington Dunbar and Lexington Douglass played others from the Central Kentucky area with much success. Indeed, national championships found their way to Lexington through the KNAA. The dissolution of the KNAA did nothing to harm the reputations of Dunbar and Douglass, as they regularly competed and held their own with the other schools in Fayette County. Dunbar even finished as state runner-up twice.

The dissolution of some schools and the creation of new ones have seen schools in Fayette County gain larger enrollments, and with new opposition, new rivalries are created. Athens, St. Catherine's Academy, Lexington Latin, and University High have all become memories as high schools, although most of them have affiliations with new schools—in particular, Bryan Station and Lexington Catholic—to continue the tradition.

The creation of Tates Creek in 1965 and Paul Laurence Dunbar in 1990 were both necessary because of the city of Lexington's expansion, and both added an extra challenge to the local basketball scene. New rivalries were forged, and the schools soon represented the area in the state tournament, both having reached the final.

Since 2000, Fayette County teams have been extremely strong, with two state championships and many highly ranked teams, some at the national level. The future looks bright for local teams. Maybe another book can be produced similar to this one in 50 to 60 years, and the players of today can look through its pages and take a stroll down their memory lane.

1

Before 1950

A rare photograph shows the basketball team from the 1920–1921 season representing Model High School. The school would eventually change its name to become University High. (Courtesy of Gene Huff.)

The starting five for Lexington High School pose for a photograph prior to the 1921–1922 season. The team went on to win the state championship, defeating Frankfort 55-7 in the final. (Courtesy of Henry Clay High School.)

The players of the 1925–1926 Lexington High School basketball team are photographed on the steps of the school prior to the start of the season. (Courtesy of Henry Clay High School.)

Pictured is the trophy won by the 1929–1930 Dunbar Bearcats for becoming the champions of the Negro High School State Tournament. The trophy is inscribed, "State Champions 1930, Dunbar Bearcats" and goes on to name the squad as follows: C. Livisay, N. Guy, L. Shiddell, J. Livingston, J. Jones, W. Hall, and coach F. L. Baker. The trophy is currently held on display in the Dunbar Alumni Room at Paul Laurence Dunbar High School. (Photograph by Kismet Photography, courtesy of author's personal collection.)

Pictured are the players and staff of the 1929 Lexington High School basketball team. Although the lineup order is not known, those pictured are Evans D. Tracy, Norbert Campbell, Erle Powell, Ralph Kercheval, Robert Hickey, Tom Foley, Maurice Jackson, manager John D. Freeman, and head coach John G. Heber. (Courtesy of Henry Clay High School.)

Lexington High School's team for the 1927–1928 season poses for the photographer prior to the start of the season. It is interesting to note the size of the squad compared to those of previous seasons. (Courtesy of Henry Clay High School.)

The 1930–1931 Athens Tigers pose for a photograph. (Courtesy of Bob Baesler.)

Pictured are the players of the Henry Clay basketball team as depicted in their school's quarterly magazine, the *Hi-Times*, in 1934. (Courtesy of Henry Clay High School.)

This photograph shows action from a Henry Clay game during the 1935–1936 season. The Blue Devils advanced to the regional final, where they were defeated 26-25 by Midway. (Courtesy of Henry Clay High School.)

Henry Clay's team poses for a photograph prior to the 1935–1936 season. Although the actual lineup is not available, the squad included head coach John Heber, Eldon Sloan, Mason Johnson, Omer Cunningham, Frank Wilford, John Boles, Sherry Blumer, Billy Bell, Dan Terrell, Vernon Trammel, Raymond Wallace, Harold Dever, and Robert Abney. (Courtesy of Henry Clay High School.)

2

THE 1950S

The 1949–1950 Lafayette Generals pose with a trophy, possibly the district or regional title, as the team finished the season as state champions by defeating Clark County in the final by a score of 55-51. (Courtesy of author's personal collection.)

The 1952–1953 Athens Tigers pose for a squad photograph. From left to right are (first row) Bobby Eades, Charlie Crosby, Bobby Guilfoil, Eddie Townsend, Tommy Johns, and Dale Turner; (second row) Raymond Hayes, Bob Baesler, David Brumagen, Bradley Rhorer, Howard Blakeman, and head coach Bob Abney. (Courtesy of Bob Baesler.)

The Lexington Catholic Knights prepare for the 1952–1953 season. Pictured from left to right are (first row) manager Billy Hickey, (second row) John Greely, Sonny Tibbs, Glen Merriman, Joe Webster, and Paul Frank; (third row) head coach Nick Wanchic, Frank Schwendeman, Joe Fister, Paul Armstrong, Jude Zwick, John Duffy, and athletic director Rev. Fredrick Bamberger. (Courtesy of Lexington Catholic High School.)

The program cover for the 1953 43rd District Tournament shows that the event took place at Memorial Coliseum in Lexington and was hosted by University High. Lafayette won the tournament on the way to winning the state championship. (Courtesy of Bob Baesler.)

The 1953 state champion Lafayette Generals pose for a pre-season photograph. Pictured from left to right are (first row) assistant manager Bud Dickens, Steve Shuck, Jackie Terrill, Walter Newton, Norris Flynn, Tommy Wallin, and assistant manager Eddie Crutcher; (second row) student manager Jimmy Rollins, trainer Jerry Werner, Erroll Cooper, Don Plunkett, Vernon Hatton, Bill Florence, John Peck, Edd Stipp, Doug Shively, and head coach Ralph Carlisle. (Courtesy of Bob Baesler.)

The cagers of Henry Clay ready themselves for the 1953–1954 season. Pictured from left to right are (first row) Vic Thorndale, Bobby Kidd, Art McClanahan, and Lee Rose; (second row) Stanley Huffman, David Bader, Allen Grimes, and Edgar Rust; (third row) head coach Elmer Gilb, Phil Fritz, Douglass Blair, ? Williams, and manager Don Elliott. (Courtesy of Billy Guilfoil.)

The Knights of Lexington Catholic pose for a photograph during the 1953–1954 season. Pictured from left to right are (first row) Lou Swift, Billy Barrett, Jimmy McGurk, manager Robert Mueller, and Tom Hunt; (second row) David Milliken, John Meyer, Jim Lynch, and Bud Greely; (third row) Paul Frank, Mike DeBoor, Dick Garland, Sonny Tibbs, Tim Scully, Bill Greely, and head coach Nick Wanchic. (Courtesy of Billy Guilfoil.)

The University Heights 1953–1954 squad are pictured together. From left to right are (first row) Skipper Adams, Billy Heinz, David Whitehouse, Tommy Ginger, T. Kinkead, Billy Ginger, Lawrence Yates, and Thomas Rich; (second row) Joe Hagin, Ken Brown, Phil Johnson, W. R. Brown, James Fortenberry, Jim Farris, and manager Jimmy Whittenberg. The Purples had a regular season record of 15 wins and 4 losses under the leadership of head coach King Richeson. (Courtesy of Billy Guilfoil.)

Athens head coach Bob Abney (left) holds the Bluegrass Conference's Sutcliffe Trophy with player Bob Baesler in 1955. (Courtesy of Bob Baesler.)

The squad members of Lafayette's 1954–1955 season included, from left to right, (first row) Gerald Denny, Rankin Blount Jr., Freddie Brown, Harold Buffin, Sonny Cobb, Billy Dickerson, Donald Hopper, Eddie Sellier, and Lary Heath; (second row) Nolan Carter Jr., Don Duvall, James Kays, Doug Shively, Billy Ray Lickert, Ronnie Hacker, and Gerald Walton; (third row) trainer John Fernandez, manager Bill McGoodwin, Frank Martin, Billy Agger, Mitchell True, manager Eddie Crutcher, and manager Raymond Wafford. (Courtesy of Billy Guilfoil.)

The 1954–1955 Athens Tigers pose for a pre-season photograph. Pictured from left to right are (first row) head coach Bob Abney, Tommy Johns, Pete Dailey, Eddie Townsend, Kelley Lawson, and Ike Thompson; (second row) J. B. Wingate, Luther Stivers, Bobby English, Bob Baesler, Howard Blakeman, Billy Guilfoil, and manager John Kelley. (Courtesy of Billy Guilfoil.)

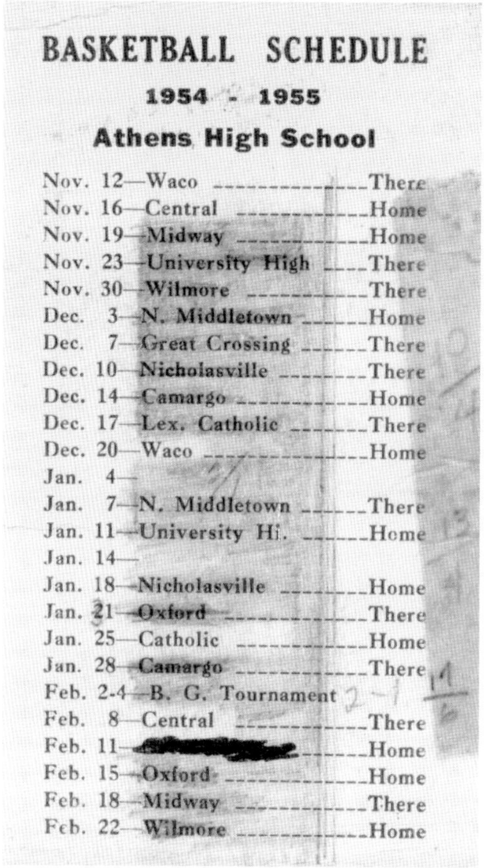

BASKETBALL SCHEDULE

1954 - 1955

Athens High School

Date	Opponent	Site
Nov. 12	Waco	There
Nov. 16	Central	Home
Nov. 19	Midway	Home
Nov. 23	University High	There
Nov. 30	Wilmore	There
Dec. 3	N. Middletown	Home
Dec. 7	Great Crossing	There
Dec. 10	Nicholasville	There
Dec. 14	Camargo	Home
Dec. 17	Lex. Catholic	There
Dec. 20	Waco	Home
Jan. 4		
Jan. 7	N. Middletown	There
Jan. 11	University Hi.	Home
Jan. 14		
Jan. 18	Nicholasville	Home
Jan. 21	Oxford	There
Jan. 25	Catholic	Home
Jan. 28	Camargo	There
Feb. 2-4	B. G. Tournament	
Feb. 8	Central	There
Feb. 11	[illegible]	Home
Feb. 15	Oxford	Home
Feb. 18	Midway	There
Feb. 22	Wilmore	Home

Pictured is a 1954–1955 schedule for Athens. Notice how many of the teams named here, in addition to Athens, are no longer in existence. (Courtesy of Bob Baesler.)

Below, posing for a preseason photograph is the 1955–1956 University High team. Pictured from left to right are (first row) manager John O'Dear, Jim Breakfield, Bill Taylor, Lanny Cox, Sam Ward, Bradley Switzer, ? Swartz, and ? Williams; (second row) manager John Kaltenborn, Ernest Clarke, B. Ginger, W. R. Brown, Worley Harper, Tommy Ginger, and Charles Maxson. Coached by Ed Shemelya, the Purples had a record of 6-9 going into district play. (Courtesy of Gene Huff.)

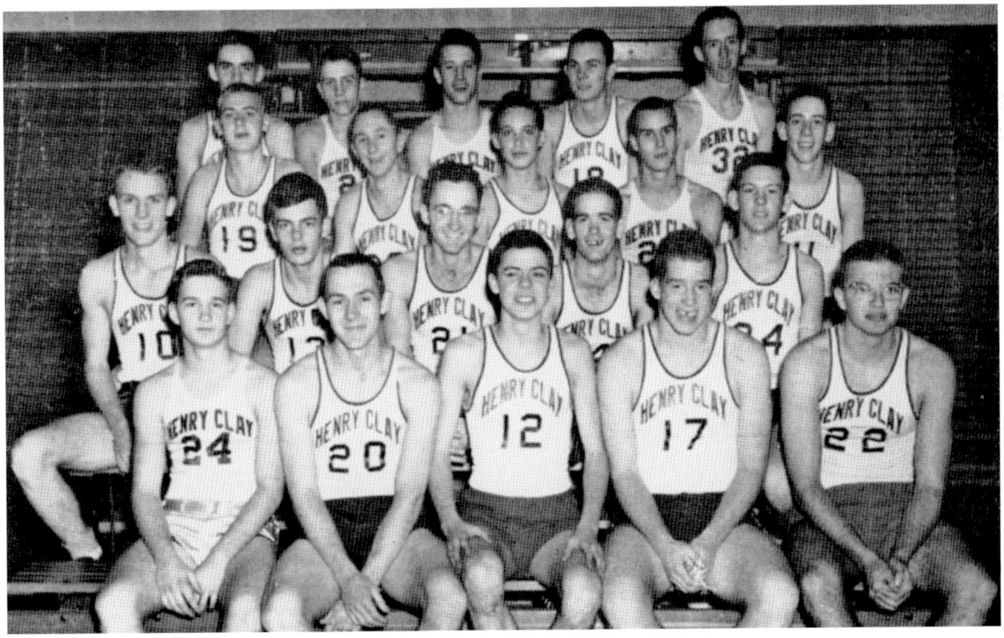

The Blue Devils of Henry Clay pose for a photograph during the 1955–1956 season. From left to right are (first row) Jimmy Lentz, Jack Massie, Roger Gum, Brit Kirwan, and Fred Hynson; (second row) Charles Owen, William Bader, George Wigglesworth, ? Agee, and ? McDowell; (third row) Robert Craig, Ben Zimmerman, Charles Waller, David Wilson, and ? Ades; (fourth row) Bobby Jones, John Colyer, Delza Maggard, Okie Nelson, and ? Banta. (Courtesy of Billy Guilfoil.)

The Douglass Demons of 1956–1957 pose for a photograph. From left to right are James Benton, George Bell, Henry Bell, Kenneth Logan, Lyman Jones, John Burdette, Paul Price, Robert Shye, Delbert Watkins, Waller Edwards, Andrew Fisher, and Kenneth Spotts. (Courtesy of Billy Guilfoil.)

The 1956–1957 version of Lexington Catholic's Knights are pictured. From left to right are (first row) Jim McGurk, Gene Thompson, Leonard Brown, and manager Bob Warren; (second row) head coach Nick Wanchic, manager David Tramontin, Charles Hitchinson, Lewis Swift, and Jim DeVries; (third row) Bobby Grant, Joe Patrick, Joe Warren, Tony Schweighardt, and Rabe Moloney. (Courtesy of Billy Guilfoil.)

Coached by S. T. Roach, the Dunbar Bearcats had a reputation for having strong teams. Pictured here is the 1956–1957 version of the Bearcats. From left to right are (first row) Robert Jackson, Alan Hardin, Alvinus White, Samuel Adams, Roger Byrd, and Thyrone Henderson; (second row) Willie Jackson, James Taylor, Richard Johnson, Julius Berry, James Hampton, Robert Burbage, and Felix Scruggs. (Courtesy of Billy Guilfoil.)

The 1957 43rd District Tournament in was hosted by University Heights and was played at the University of Kentucky Coliseum. Six Fayette County schools participated in this tournament, namely Lafayette, University High, Dunbar, Henry Clay, Athen, and Lexington Catholic. (Courtesy of Billy Guilfoil.)

Official Program

UNIVERSITY HIGH

Hosts to the

1957 43rd District

Basketball Tournament

★

University of Kentucky Coliseum

FEBRUARY 27, 28, MARCH 1, 2

This photograph of the 1956–1957 Lafayette Generals was taken from the district tournament program. The Generals went on to become state champions. Pictured from left to right are (first row) trainer Harold Moberly, manager John Gerlach, Jimmy Whitmore, Art West, Dallous Reed, Don Duvall, Bobby Newsome, manager Billy Hammond, and manager Sam Downing; (second row) head coach Ralph Carlisle, Frank Martin, Mitchell True, Gerald Denny, Dave Filer, Billy Ray Lickert, Tim Thompson, Freddie Brown, and coach Ken Caudill. (Courtesy of Billy Guilfoil.)

1958 All-State Basketball Team

This is to certify that

SCOTTY BAESLER, Athens High School,

is a member of The Courier-Journal All-State High School Basketball Team, chosen by a board made up of coaches, sports writers and officials in the Commonwealth of Kentucky.

Earl Cox
Earl Cox, Chairman
All-State Committee

Earl Ruby
Earl Ruby
Sports Editor

Scotty Baesler of Athens High School was selected as an All-State Team member in 1958. Pictured here is the certificate he received from the All-State Committee. (Courtesy of Scotty Baesler.)

This action shot is from a game during Bryan Station's first season, 1958–1959. (Courtesy of Bryan Station High School.)

Pictured here is the first basketball team to represent Bryan Station High School in the 1958–1959 season. Pictured from left to right are (first row) Jimmy Sabo, Dickie Kingsland, Tommy Southworth, Ronnie Gayheart, Billy Mullins, Boyd Elliott, Raymond Rhorer, and manager Kenny Roy; (second row) reserve coach Tom Updike, Jimmy Lynch, Don Berger, Albert Mitchell, Bill Stewart, Edmond Stone, Scotty Baesler, and head coach Bob Abney; (third row) manager Claude Rhorer, manager Steve Barnett, Preston Price, Charles Williams, Billy Allison, Larry Measle, Coby Barker, and Bob Rineman. (Courtesy of Bryan Station High School.)

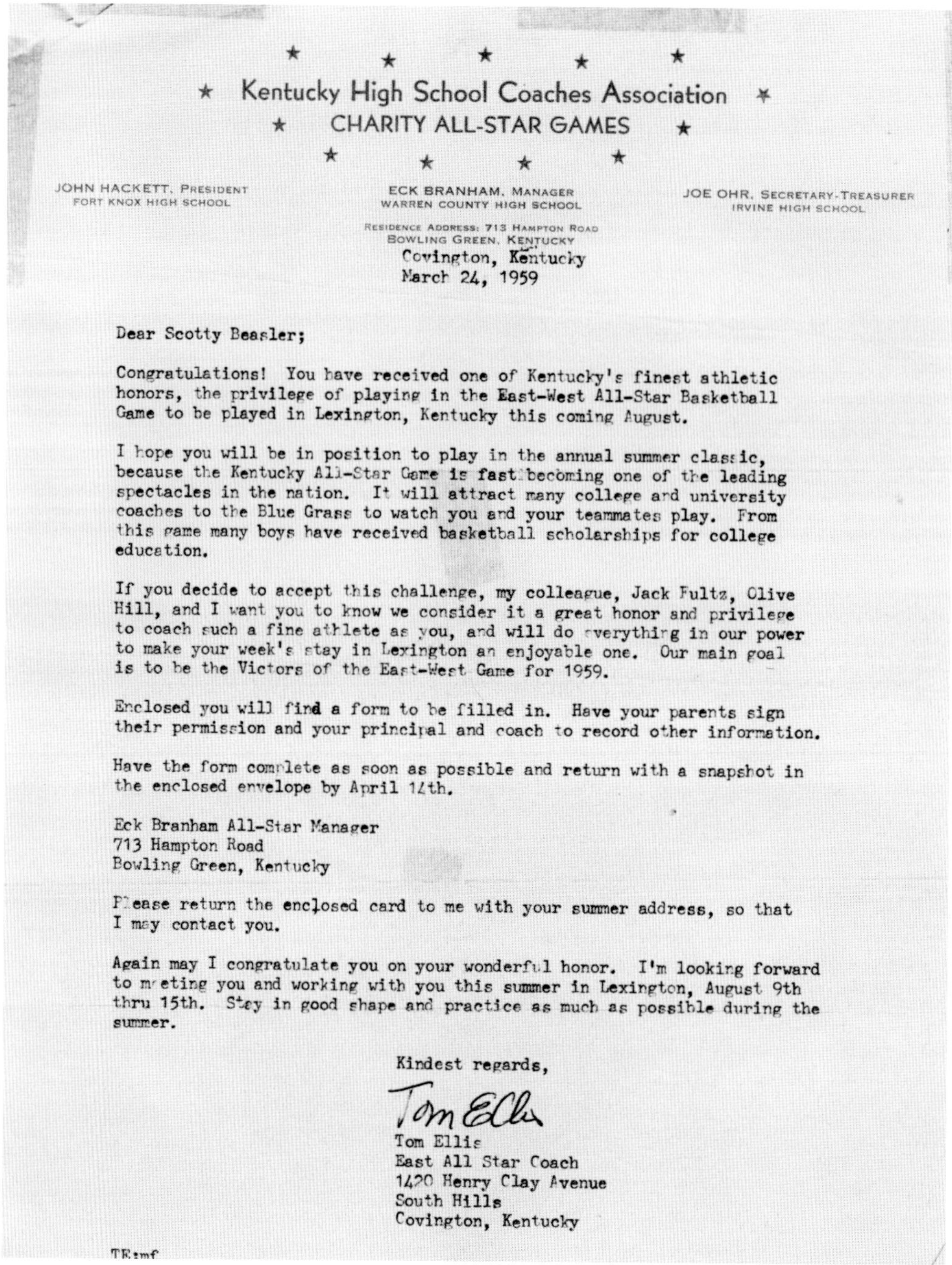

★ Kentucky High School Coaches Association ★
★ CHARITY ALL-STAR GAMES ★

JOHN HACKETT, PRESIDENT
FORT KNOX HIGH SCHOOL

ECK BRANHAM, MANAGER
WARREN COUNTY HIGH SCHOOL

JOE OHR, SECRETARY-TREASURER
IRVINE HIGH SCHOOL

RESIDENCE ADDRESS: 713 HAMPTON ROAD
BOWLING GREEN, KENTUCKY

Covington, Kentucky
March 24, 1959

Dear Scotty Beasler;

Congratulations! You have received one of Kentucky's finest athletic honors, the privilege of playing in the East-West All-Star Basketball Game to be played in Lexington, Kentucky this coming August.

I hope you will be in position to play in the annual summer classic, because the Kentucky All-Star Game is fast becoming one of the leading spectacles in the nation. It will attract many college and university coaches to the Blue Grass to watch you and your teammates play. From this game many boys have received basketball scholarships for college education.

If you decide to accept this challenge, my colleague, Jack Fultz, Olive Hill, and I want you to know we consider it a great honor and privilege to coach such a fine athlete as you, and will do everything in our power to make your week's stay in Lexington an enjoyable one. Our main goal is to be the Victors of the East-West Game for 1959.

Enclosed you will find a form to be filled in. Have your parents sign their permission and your principal and coach to record other information.

Have the form complete as soon as possible and return with a snapshot in the enclosed envelope by April 14th.

Eck Branham All-Star Manager
713 Hampton Road
Bowling Green, Kentucky

Please return the enclosed card to me with your summer address, so that I may contact you.

Again may I congratulate you on your wonderful honor. I'm looking forward to meeting you and working with you this summer in Lexington, August 9th thru 15th. Stay in good shape and practice as much as possible during the summer.

Kindest regards,

Tom Ellis

Tom Ellis
East All Star Coach
1420 Henry Clay Avenue
South Hills
Covington, Kentucky

TE:mf

Bryan Station's Scotty Baesler was selected to play in the prestigious East-West All-Star game in 1959. Pictured here is the letter Baesler received informing him of his selection. (Courtesy of Scotty Baesler.)

3

THE 1960s

The Purples of University High pose for a team photograph prior to the 1960–1961 season. Pictured from left to right are (first row) managers Robert Milward and Tommy Adams; (second row) Joe Goodwin, Bill Stoll, Wink Shier, Brint Milward, Bill Turnbull, Karl Eldridge, Jim Coolsen, and Bruce Davis; (third row) Linn Litkenhous, Jan Gadjik, Joe Miller, Lyle Walker, Robert Walker, Buddy Bishop, Mike Cox, Garland Barr, David Switzer, and head coach Gene Huff. (Courtesy of Gene Huff.)

Mike Cox (33) of University High awaits a rebound among a bevy of Lexington Catholic defenders while his teammate, Buddy Bishop (22), looks on during a game from the 1960–1961 season. The referee to the left of the picture is a young C. M. Newton, a future athletic director at the University of Kentucky. (Courtesy of Gene Huff.)

Bryan Station's Kenny Mahanes (23) and Albert Mitchell (31) harass a Frankfort player in this action shot taken during the 1960–1961 season. (Courtesy of Bryan Station High School.)

Bryan Station's starting center during the 1960–1961 season was 6-foot, 7-inch Bill Allison, pictured here scoring a basket during a practice session. (Courtesy of Bryan Station High School.)

Shown below is action from a game between the Dunbar Bearcats and the St. Xavier Tigers played on February 23, 1962. St. Xavier defeated Dunbar 79-57 and eventually went on to become state champions for that season. (Courtesy of author's personal collection.)

Robert Thurston (13) of Bryan Station challenges a Franklin County player for the ball and is fouled in the process. The Defenders played the Flyers twice during the 1962–1963 season, emerging victorious both times by scores of 85-69 and 52-46. (Courtesy of Bryan Station High School.)

Henry Clay's 1962–1963 team poses for a photograph. Pictured from left to right are (first row) Curtis Carter, Doug Willoughby, Philip Bloomfield, Gene Sayre, Philip Blumer, and manager James Robinson; (second row) coach Al Prewitt, Ronnie Carter, Sam Cox, Lewis Sutherland, Ronnie Cox, Manlius Neal, Bobby Atkinson, Bill Nickell, Van Alford, B. Roberts, and assistant coach Hunter Durham. This was Coach Prewitt's first season in charge of the Blue Devils, and he led them to a 17-7 record. (Courtesy of Henry Clay High School.)

Lafayette's Al Torstrick loses control of the basketball in a game against Henry Clay during the 1962–1963 season. The two schools only met once that season, with the Lafayette Generals winning by a score of 41-35. Torstrick scored 22 points in the game. (Courtesy of author's personal collection.)

Lafayette's Mark Trumbo (14) battles for a rebound with two Bryan Station Defenders in a game during the 1962–1963 season. Lafayette won the game 68-52. (Courtesy of author's personal collection.)

P. J. Bloomfield (15) and Sam Cox (23) attempt to gather the ball in front of Bryan Station's Tommy Gray (23) during the 1962–1963 season. Henry Clay defeated Bryan Station twice that season, including a 47-40 game in the district tournament. (Courtesy of Bryan Station High School.)

Head coach Ken Caudill was in his second season at Lafayette in the 1962–1963 school year. Caudill led his team to a 15-7 record. (Courtesy of author's personal collection.)

Bryan Station's Tommy Gray (23) puts up a shot under pressure from two Franklin County Flyers while Mike Perkins (31) moves in to claim a possible rebound in this 1962–1963 clash. (Courtesy of Bryan Station High School.)

Henry Clay's Lewis Sutherland (20) and Van Alford (31) fight for a rebound in a game against Lafayette during the 1962–1963 season. Lafayette went on to win the game 41-35 on its home court. (Courtesy of Henry Clay High School.)

This photograph depicts the view from behind the Defenders' bench as Bryan Station's Clifford Wilson shoots against the Franklin County Flyers in the 1962–1963 season. (Courtesy of Bryan Station High School.)

Lafayette (white) and Dunbar tip off in the second round of the 1963 district tournament. Dunbar would go on to win the game 32-21. (Courtesy of author's personal collection.)

Henry Clay's Curtis Carter (10) and Van Alford (23) fight two Lexington Catholic opponents for a rebound during the 1963–1964 season. (Courtesy of Henry Clay High School.)

Pictured below are Henry Clay's starting five for the 1963–1964 season along with their coach. From left to right are Manlius Neal (14), Van Alford (23), head coach Al Prewitt, Robert Atkinson (22), Malcolm Willoughby (11), and Curtis Carter (10). (Courtesy of Henry Clay High School.)

James Barry challenges the tip-off for Bryan Station in a game at Bourbon County during the 1963–1964 season. Bryan Station lost three times to the Colonels that season by scores of 77-42, 77-72, and 70-61. (Courtesy of Bryan Station High School.)

Henry Clay's James Wilkes and Manlius Neal (14) challenge an unidentified Lexington Catholic player for the ball in a game during the 1963–1964 season. (Courtesy of Henry Clay High School.)

The Sayre team poses for a photograph at the beginning of the 1964–1965 season. From left to right are (first row) Alfred Nuckols and Jerome Johnson; (second row) Michael Frazier, John Palumbo, Barry Hall, Larry Flynn, Toll Hollingsworth, and Charles Beasley; (third row) coach Norris Flynn, William Schwert, Richard Meyers, Madison Cawein, Charles Stone, Denzil Hollingsworth, Clinton Hancock, and assistant coach John Kelley. (Courtesy of Sayre School.)

The University High team poses for a photograph before the 1964–1965 season. Pictured from left to right are (first row) manager Hal Scott, Tommy Adams, Jimmy Pyle, Rodger Baker, Bob Kennoy, and manager Mike Gurnee; (second row) head coach Gene Huff, Don Musselman, Bill Ready, Sam Brown, Mike Maddox, and Jim Alcorn. (Courtesy of Gene Huff.)

Bruce Davis (42) of University High puts up a shot against Powell County while Carl Eldridge (45) looks on during the 1964–1965 season. The two teams played each other twice that season, with University High taking the first meeting by a score of 85-69 while the return game ended in a rare tie, 64-64. (Courtesy of Gene Huff.)

Bryan Station's Defenders pose for a photograph prior to the 1964–1965 season. Pictured from left to right are (first row) manager Michael Casey, captain Robert Berry, head coach Bob Abney, captain Duaine Clark, and manager Mike Ruehling; (second row) manager Steven Abney, John McClelland, Billy Hilliard, Grant Robinson, D. Lunsford, John Fuller, Morris Engles, Ronnie Campbell, Hannibal Ware, James Ware, Kenny Patrick, and assistant coach D. Jones. (Courtesy of Bryan Station High School.)

Bryan Station's Kenny Patrick (12) pushes a bounce pass through to a teammate during a game against Bourbon County in the Defenders' 1964–1965 campaign. Bryan Station played the Bourbon County Colonels three times that season, falling short on each occasion by scores of 60-53, 73-72, and 62-57. (Courtesy of Bryan Station High School.)

The Lafayette Generals of the 1964–1965 season pose for a team photograph. Pictured from left to right are (first row) manager Carl Hocker, Ronnie Duvall, Chesley Jaracz, Terry Sleet, George Hampton, Barney Hudson, John Spickard, Doug Osborne, and manager Tommy Wade; (second row) Ronnie Eades, Jack Murrell, Jim Perkins, Pug Wellman, Dan Groth, Brian Cooper, Don Fischer, Howard Mullendore, Bill Taylor, and head coach Herky Rupp. (Courtesy of author's personal collection.)

Lafayette's George Hampton shoots a layup in a game against the Ashland Tomcats during the 1964–1965 season. (Courtesy of author's personal collection.)

An unidentified Tates Creek player shoots for two points in a game during the school's first season of basketball in 1965–1966. (Courtesy of Tates Creek High School.)

Bryan Station's Ken Curry (31) gets a shot off over the attempted block of a visiting Pendleton County player during the 1965–1966 season. Bryan Station would finish the contest on the losing end by a score of 67-61. (Courtesy of Bryan Station High School.)

The Sayre Spartans win the tip-off in a game during the 1965–1966 season. (Courtesy of Sayre School.)

The Sayre Spartans ready themselves for the 1966–1967 season. Pictured from left to right are (first row) Jon Demos, Bill Cowgill, Shan Wolfram, and Robert McCray; (second row) Toll Hollingsworth, Tom Sayre, Berry Hall, and Clinton Hancock; (third row) Steve Ruschell, Craig Reynolds, John Palumbo, and Larry Flynn. (Courtesy of Sayre School.)

The Bryan Station team of the 1966–1967 campaign is pictured prior to the start of the season. (Courtesy of Bryan Station High School.)

Players from Bryan Station (white) and Lafayette challenge for a loose ball in a game between the schools during the 1966–1967 season. (Courtesy of Bryan Station High School.)

Sayre's Craig Reynolds gets a shot off in a game against Louisville Country Day during the 1966–1967 season. The two schools played each other no less than three times that season, with the Spartans the victors in only the final meeting by a score of 77-43. (Courtesy of Sayre School.)

Tates Creek students have a message for the Lafayette fans as they show their school spirit during the 1967–1968 season. (Courtesy of Tates Creek High School.)

Rodney Brewer (44) and Hank List (22) of Tates Creek challenge an unidentified Lexington Catholic player for a rebound during the 1967–1968 season. The Tates Creek Commodores defeated the Knights twice that year, including an 86-59 victory in the first round of the 43rd District Tournament. (Courtesy of Tates Creek High School.)

The Henry Clay and Frankfort centers battle for the tip-off in a contest between the two schools during the 1968–1969 season. The teams encountered each other twice that season, with Henry Clay taking the honors in both games by scores of 62-60 and 63-61. (Courtesy of Henry Clay High School.)

The Tates Creek team of 1968–1969 includes, from left to right, (first row) Phil Latham, Danny Mingo, Ben Ferrell, Jim Slabaugh, Aaron "Boo" Carter, Donald Williams, Richard Roberts, Kenneth Littrell, and Gene Sageser; (second row) Steve Musgrave, Mike Lewis, Marvin Walker, Richard Floyd, Dave McIntosh, Bill Thompson, Jim Cook, Fred Nelson, and S. Slabaugh; (third row) Steve Shuey, Donnie Woods, Craig Wilkie, Dennis Smith, Dwaine Parsons, Rodney Brewer, Richard Smith, Theodore Jackson, Paul Ferrell, and Ricky Cooper. (Courtesy of Tates Creek High School.)

Players from the Henry Clay (dark) and Tates Creek teams challenge for a rebound in a game between the two teams during the 1968–1969 season. The schools met three times during the campaign with the regular-season games being split, 64-63 to Tates Creek and 68-66 to Henry Clay. The Tates Creek Commodores defeated the Blue Devils in a third encounter, a 72-61 win in the district tournament, to end Henry Clay's season. (Courtesy of Tates Creek High School.)

Dennis Smith goes up for a basket for Tates Creek during the 1968–1969 season. Smith finished the season as the leading scorer in Lexington, in addition to being named to the AP Sports Writers' First Team, the UPI's Board of Coaches All-State Second Team, and the Kentucky All-Stars. (Courtesy of Tates Creek High School.)

Lexington Catholic's 6-foot, 8-inch center, Kent Reynolds, wins the tip-off over his Sayre counterpart in the first round of the district tournament in 1969. Lexington Catholic would win the game 66-43. (Courtesy of Sayre School.)

4

The 1970s

Tates Creek's Steve Musgrave leaves the game and puts his warm-up jacket back on for the last time as he ends his high school career with a 53-35 loss against Frankfort in the regional semifinal in 1970. (Courtesy of Tates Creek High School.)

Bryan Station's Don Davis (15) goes up for a tip-in against Lafayette during the 1969–1970 season. Davis was named to the All Mid-State Conference team that season. (Courtesy of Bryan Station High School.)

The Generals of Lafayette try to stop Bryan Station's John Garner (31) from getting his jump shot off during a game from the 1969–1970 campaign. (Courtesy of Bryan Station High School.)

Bruce Isaacs drives the ball up court for his Sayre Spartans in a game against Nicholas County during the 1969–1970 season. (Courtesy of Sayre School.)

Craig Wilkie rises above the Mason County defense in a game during the 1969–1970 season. Wilkie ended the year as Tates Creek's most valuable player and assists leader. (Courtesy of Tates Creek High School.)

Tates Creek senior Marvin Walker leaps above an unidentified Bryan Station player to gather a rebound during the 1970–1971 season. The Bryan Station Defenders finished on the losing end of both contests with the Commodores that year, going down 56-52 and 81-56. (Courtesy of Tates Creek High School.)

An unidentified Bryan Station player is pressured by Steve Shuey (20) and Donnie Williams during a game in the 1969–1970 season. Bryan Station won both times its team faced Tates Creek that season by scores of 62-53 and 59-53. (Courtesy of Tates Creek High School.)

Bill Silliman of Tates Creek takes the ball down the court looking for a teammate to pass to in a 1970–1971 game against Madison County. Tates Creek won the game 73-58. (Courtesy of Tates Creek High School.)

The Bryan Station Defenders are pictured before a successful 1971–1972 basketball season. Pictured from left to right are (first row) manager Jeff Sharp and manager Charles Mitchell; (second row) Buck Clay, Carl Hubbard, James Clay, Louis McDowell, Jack Givens, Carl Shye, Ted Hundley, Butch Washington, Melvin Sykes, Eddie Neal, Ron Birch, Sam Smith, Ronnie Williams, and Paul Morgan. (Courtesy of Bryan Station High School.)

Bryan Station sophomore Jack Givens leaps for the layup in a 1972 district tournament game against rivals Lafayette. The Defenders defeated the Lafayette Generals 85-51 on their way to winning both the 43rd District and 11th Region titles. (Courtesy of Bryan Station High School.)

The Sayre Spartans varsity squad poses for a 1971–1972 team picture. Pictured from left to right are (first row) manager John Gott, Brad Good, Mike Rose, Jimmy Richmond, Tom Cowgill, and Rusty Milburn; (second row) coach Larry Martin, Don Rardin, Mike Wilson, Wayne Williams, Guy Harris, Joe Ripley, Chris Puffer, Ike Lawrence, and coach Gerald Walton. The team ended the season with a 20-4 record. (Courtesy of Sayre School.)

Bryan Station's trio of coaches, (from left to right) Charles Livisay, Bob Barlow, and Ed Allin, watch the action during the 1971–1972 season. They would lead their Defenders to the semifinals of the state tournament at Louisville's Freedom Hall, where they would lose 67-63 to the eventual state champions, Owensboro. (Courtesy of Bryan Station High School.)

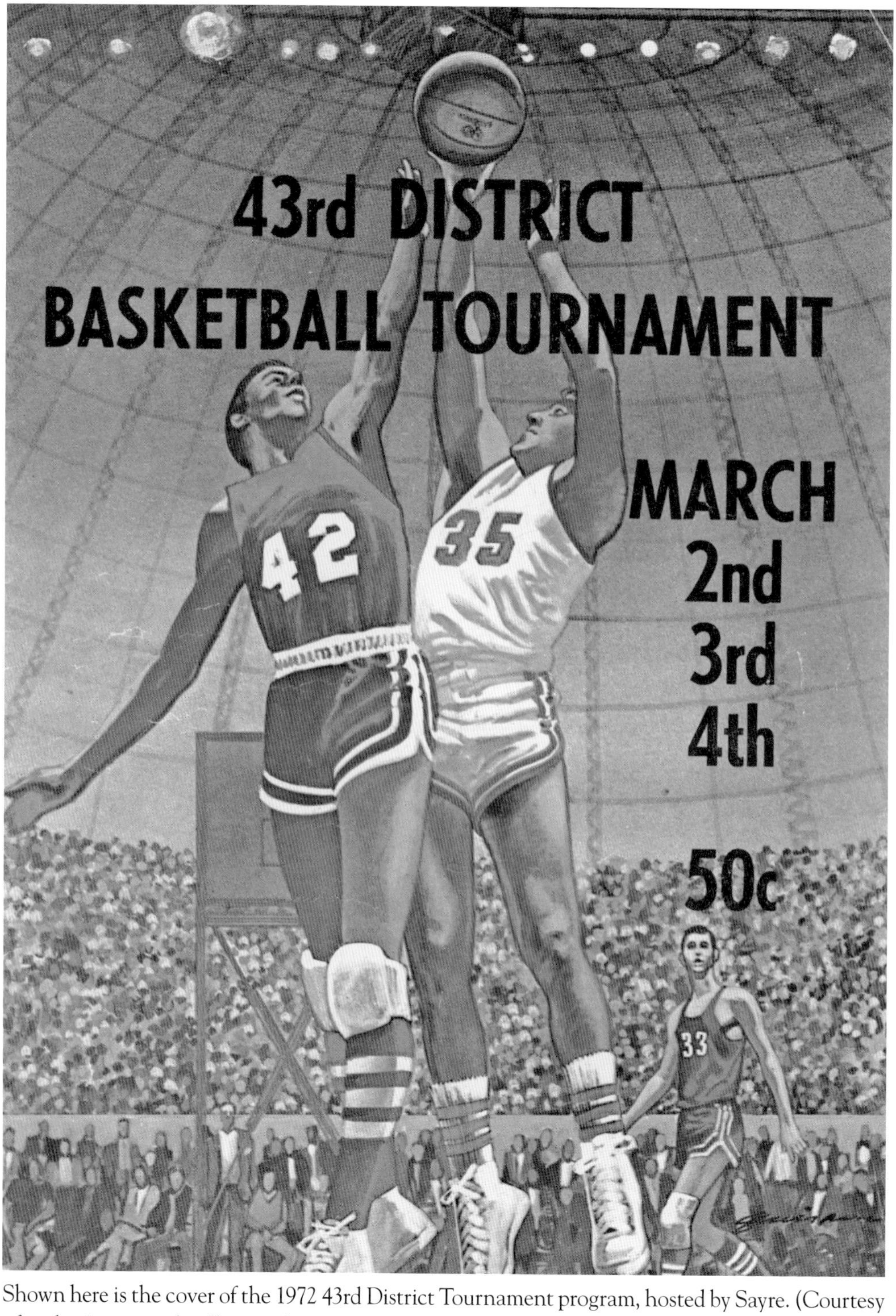

Shown here is the cover of the 1972 43rd District Tournament program, hosted by Sayre. (Courtesy of author's personal collection.)

The cover of the program for a game played between Lafayette and Henry Clay at the Lafayette Gymnasium on December 22, 1972, is pictured. Programs for individual games between schools are rare. (Courtesy of author's personal collection.)

Mark Rawlings (14) rises above a Henry Clay rival to gather a rebound for Tates Creek while teammate Eric Singleton looks on during the 1972–1973 season. (Courtesy of Tates Creek High School.)

James Clay (15) drives past a Franklin County opponent on his way to the basket for Bryan Station during the 1972–1973 season. (Courtesy of Bryan Station High School.)

Sayre's Jimmy Richmond has his shot blocked by a Harrodsburg player during the 1972–1973 season. Harrodsburg went on to win the game played at Sayre by a score of 77-75. Sayre would finish the season with a 10-15 record. (Courtesy of Sayre School.)

Donnie Rardin (31) puts a shot up for his Bryan Station team in a game against Lafayette during the 1972–1973 season. (Courtesy of Bryan Station High School.)

The Lexington Catholic team of 1972–1973 put together a 18-15 season. The team is pictured here, from left to right: assistant coach Rev. Robert Nieberding, manager Ricky Starns, John O'Brien, Steve Tattershall, Kelly Weir, Donny Locknane, Jesse Caudill, David Kuykendall, Joe Wombwell, Bill Rambicure, Pat Payne, Charlie Riddell, Johnny Houston, David Wehrle, John Hinkel, Roger Searcy, manager Mark Hopkins, and head coach Tommy Starns. (Courtesy of Lexington Catholic High School.)

Bryan Station's Jack Givens (21) beats two Tates Creek players to the rebound in a game from the 1972–1973 campaign. Tates Creek defeat the Defenders three times that year by scores of 45-42, 54-52, and 60-55, the latter being the semifinal of the 43rd District Tournament. (Courtesy of Bryan Station High School.)

The 1973–1974 Bryan Station basketball team went 30-5 on the season, claimed the Fayette County Invitational Tournament and the Louisville Invitational Tournament, won both the 43rd District and 11th Region titles, and made the second round of the state tournament. The team is pictured prior to that illustrious season. From left to right are (first row) Kenny Thompson, Pat Littleton, Donnie Moore, Norman Jackson, Buck Clay, Odyncy Johnson, Stewart Beatty, and Perry Noplis; (second row) coach Bob Barlow, coach Charles Livisay, Robin Parker, James Clay, Jack Givens, Jim Hodge, Glenn Taylor, Anthony Jackson, and coach Ed Allin. (Courtesy of Bryan Station High School.)

Action from the 1973–1974 Bryan Station–Tates Creek game includes Anthony Jackson (23) thwarting a scoring attempt by an unidentified Tates Creek Commodore. (Courtesy of Bryan Station High School.)

James Clay (15) drives to the basket for Bryan Station in a 1973–1974 game against Lafayette. The Defenders emerged victorious from both contests against the Lafayette Generals that season, winning 106-69 and 65-46. (Courtesy of Bryan Station High School.)

Lexington Catholic's team poses for a photograph prior to the 1973–1974 season. Pictured from left to right are (first row) manager Ricky Starns, Gary Doyle, John Feltman, Jesse Caudill, Danny Kragel, Tom Burns, and manager Mark Hopkins; (second row) head coach Tommy Starns, Roger Searcy, Kelly Weir, Dave Kuykendall, John O'Brien, Bill Rambicure, Pat Dayne, Dave Wehrle, Jim Young, Donny Locknane, assistant coach Steve Gilmore, and statistician Barbara Higgins. (Courtesy of Lexington Catholic High School.)

Bryan Station's Jack Givens (21) dominates the backboard in a 1973–1974 game against Sayre. Givens finished his senior year with a scoring average of 25.2 points per game, the best in Lexington. He was also selected as an All-American and All-State, and was chosen as Kentucky's Mr. Basketball. (Courtesy of Bryan Station High School.)

Bill Rombauer (24) puts up a shot against Franklin County during the 1973–1974 season. Tom Burns (12), Danny Haney (52), and Gary Doyle (14) follow the play for Lexington Catholic. (Courtesy of Lexington Catholic High School.)

Kevin Reid of Sayre battles for a loose ball against an unidentified Lexington Catholic player during the 1974–1975 campaign. (Courtesy of Sayre School.)

Stewart Beatty (11) is watched by his Bryan Station teammates as he takes his turn to cut down the nets after the Defenders' 79-63 victory over Henry Clay in the 11th Region championship game. (Courtesy of Bryan Station High School.)

David Dabney (22) rises above the Henry Clay defense to get a shot off for Bryan Station in a game during the 1974–1975 season. (Courtesy of Bryan Station High School.)

Bryan Station and Tates Creek tip-off in the former's home gymnasium during the 1975–1976 season. The schools met three times that season, with the Bryan Station Defenders taking the honors each time by scores of 61-53, 70-67, and 65-63. (Courtesy of Tates Creek High School.)

Elton Bailey (35) goes up for a shot as his Bryan Station team battles Lexington Catholic in a game during the 1976–1977 campaign. The two schools met twice that season, with the Lexington Catholic Knights taking the first encounter 69-65, but the Defenders gained revenge later in the year by a score of 81-61. (Courtesy of Bryan Station High School.)

Below, posing for a team photograph prior to the 1976–1977 season are the players of the Sayre Spartan squad. From left to right are (first row) Stan Eldridge, Mike Dawahare, Rick Queen, and Steve Ballard; (second row) Mark Saunier, Bob Besten, Jeff Cole, Bill Summerlin, Bubby McKnight, Vic Chewning, and Jim McCarty. (Courtesy of Sayre School.)

Bill Summerlin shoots a free throw for Sayre in a game against Kentucky Country Day during the 1976–1977 season. (Courtesy of Sayre School.)

Bryan Station's Keith Martin (35, partially hidden) gets a shot off despite being surrounded by four Tates Creek Commodores during a district tournament clash in 1977. Tates Creek went on to win the game by a score of 63-60. (Courtesy of Bryan Station High School.)

Lexington Catholic's Danny Rossoll (24) beats everyone to the rebound, including teammates Mark Kelder (10) and Joe Durenberger (50), in a game against Jessamine County during the 1977–1978 season. The Lexington Catholic Knights would win the high-scoring encounter 101-97. (Courtesy of Lexington Catholic High School.)

The Lexington Catholic team that played the 1977–1978 season poses for a photograph. Pictured from left to right are (first row) head coach Tommy Starns, Tommy Sherlock, Bill Thompson, Mark Kelder, Mike Botkin, Jeff Haney, Scott Riggs, Mark Lanham, and assistant coach Jim Lankster; (second row) manager Dale Fernandez, Brent Schutte, Charlie Bausch, Philip Ledbetter, Mike Keene, Joe Wurtenberger, Danny Rossoll, and Jack Thomas. (Courtesy of Lexington Catholic High School.)

Scott Wilson rises above a Madison County defender for a shot during his senior season of 1977–1978. Tates Creek went on to win this game by a score of 72-59. (Courtesy of Tates Creek High School.)

Lexington Catholic's Scott Riggs (22) challenges a Bryan Station Defender for a rebound during the game between the two in the 1978 regional tournament. Bryan Station would win the game 86-70. (Courtesy of Lexington Catholic High School.)

Below, an unidentified Sayre player releases a jump shot in a game against Calvary Christian during the 1977–1978 season. (Courtesy of Sayre School.)

Tommy Sherlock (15) finds a way around his opponent for Lexington Catholic during a game in the 1978–1979 season. (Courtesy of Lexington Catholic High School.)

Danny Rossoll (24) looks to get a shot off for Lexington Catholic in a game during the 1978–1979 season. (Courtesy of Lexington Catholic High School.)

5

The 1980s

Scott Cromwell tries to find a teammate while under pressure in a game between Tates Creek and Woodford County during the 1979–1980 season. Cromwell's Commodores registered a narrow 62-61 victory at the conclusion of this game. (Courtesy of Tates Creek High School.)

Tates Creek's center during the 1979–1980 season was 6-foot, 6-inch Tommy Simpson. Simpson is pictured claiming one of his many rebounds as Scott Cromwell (20) and an unidentified Commodore look on. (Courtesy of Tates Creek High School.)

Sayre and Nelson County tip-off in a game played during the 1979–1980 season. (Courtesy of Sayre School.)

Joe Ches (white) wins the tip-off for Sayre in a game against Williamstown during the 1980–1981 campaign. (Courtesy of Sayre School.)

Bryan Station's regular starting five take the court during a state tournament game at Rupp Arena. They are Leroy Byrd (00), unidentified (25), Jeff Clay (12), William Conner (20), and Keith Berry (31). Berry was named to the All-Tournament team. (Courtesy of Bryan Station High School.)

The Sayre Spartans pose for a team photograph prior to the 1981–1982 season. Only the suited players are named. From left to right are (first row) Keith Geoghegan, Don Bergsma, Bill Patterson, Joe Ches, Mark Reineke, Tim Newcomer, and Pep Peppiatt; (second row) Weathers Hardwick, Terry Arnold, Barry Johnson, Pat Dunn, Fred Gibbs, and Tom Cox. The team posted Sayre's first winning season since 1972. (Courtesy of Sayre School.)

The Blue Grass Baptist School squad of 1981–1982 poses for a team photograph. From left to right are (first row) Tim Carver, Tommy Rhodus, and Jack Deborde; (second row) coach Lanny Templeton, Greg Page, Mike Howard, Doug Blake, R. J. Robinson, Lamoin Adcock, Jimmy Azbill, and assistant coach Joe Best. (Courtesy of Blue Grass Baptist School.)

Sayre's Keith Geoghegan readies himself for a free throw during a game in the Spartans' 1981–1982 season. (Courtesy of Sayre School.)

The Knights of Lexington Catholic ready themselves for the 1982–83 season. Pictured from left to right are (first row) Mark Mitchell, Darrin Kinder, Kevin Buehner, Greg Houlihan, Danny Johnson, Rodney Martin, and Jim Brooks; (second row) head coach Tommy Starns, Mark Abell, Kenney Frank, Richard Collins, John Kornet, Will Welch, Tim Davis, Jeff Grayson, John Stoeckinger, and assistant coach Danny Haney. (Courtesy of Lexington Catholic High School.)

Lexington Catholic's Will Welch (44) puts up a shot in a game against Harrodsburg during the 1982–1983 season. Looking on for the Knights is Rodney Martin (11). Lexington Catholic would go on to lose this game by a score of 74-70. (Courtesy of Lexington Catholic High School.)

Ricky McMackin pulls down a rebound for Tates Creek during a game against Lexington Catholic in the 1982–1983 season. The rivals met twice during the season, with both games being won by the Tates Creek Commodores, including a 76-73 overtime classic in the 11th Region semifinal. (Courtesy of Tates Creek High School.)

Kevin Buehner (12) battles his way through the Western Hills defense in a game during the 1982–1983 season. Western Hills would finish the game having defeated the Lexington Catholic team by a score of 73-51. (Courtesy of Lexington Catholic High School.)

The Bryan Station team poses below for a photograph prior to the 1983–1984 season. From left to right are (first row) manager Steve Elsey, Keith Winn, Tim Hardin, Kim Clay, Rick Sturgeon, Othello Bell, Mark Lewis, and manager Tim Mitchell; (second row) Keith Frank, Jake Keys, Marty Evans, Bobby Newton, Ollie Bates, Mike Hundley, and Gary Allen. (Courtesy of Bryan Station High School.)

Lexington Catholic's Craig Pippen attempts to control the ball in a game against Franklin County during the 1983–1984 season. (Courtesy of Lexington Catholic High School.)

Bryan Station's senior guard Tim Hardin finishes a fast break with a layup for two points during a game in the 1983–1984 season. (Courtesy of Bryan Station High School.)

Vashon High School of St. Louis, Missouri, traveled to play Bryan Station during the 1983–1984 campaign. At the end of an exciting encounter, Bryan Station took the honors, 58-55. (Courtesy of Bryan Station High School.)

Bryan Station's junior center Bobby Newton (50) rises for this fourth-quarter tip-off in the Hillbrook Classic played against Scott County at Rupp Arena during the 1984–1985 season. Also in the picture for the Bryan Station Defenders are Kim Clay (12), Keith Winn (10), Mark Lewis (11), and Jerry Tevis (42). Scott County took the honors in this game with a score of 56-43. (Courtesy of Bryan Station High School.)

Jeff Minniefield (10) puts up a shot for Tates Creek against Berea during the 1984–1985 season while teammates Clay Green (35) and John Bates (34) ready themselves for a possible rebound. (Courtesy of Tates Creek High School.)

Lexington Catholic's Mike Mitchell slows down the play as he is pressured by a Mason County defender in the first round of the 1985 Sweet Sixteen at Rupp Arena. Mason County would win the game 68-66 to move on in the tournament. (Courtesy of Lexington Catholic High School.)

The Lexington Christian School, precursor to Lexington Christian Academy, presents their first-ever school basketball team, which played the 1985–1986 season. Pictured from left to right are (first row) Steven Ray, David Miller, Paky Kramer, Brad Beach, Bart Rendel, and Dwayne Plyman; (second row) coach David Novotney, manager Robbie Huls, Brian Cobb, Robert Ray, Sean Alcorn, Darrell Plyman, and Jason Allison. (Courtesy of Lexington Christian Academy.)

Henry Clay's Sean Sutton (20) tries to thwart the shot of Noade Day (00) in a play for Bryan Station in this 1985–1986 game. Sutton is the son of then Kentucky Wildcats coach Eddie Sutton. (Courtesy of Bryan Station High School.)

Dwayne Plyman puts a shot up for his Lexington Christian School team in a game against New Covenant Academy during the 1985–1986 season. The school was a member of the Kentucky Christian Athletic Association (KCAA) during their early years. (Courtesy of Lexington Christian Academy.)

Bobby Newton (50) lays in a shot for his Bryan Station team in a 1986 district tournament game against rivals Henry Clay. The Blue Devils would take the victory 82-72. (Courtesy of Bryan Station High School.)

This action shot is from a game between Lexington's Blue Grass Baptist School and Anchord during the 1986–1987 season. Anchord would win the game 71-53. The long warm-up pants were the garb of the day for some of the Christian schools. (Courtesy of Blue Grass Baptist School.)

This photograph shows action from a game from the 1987–1988 season between Sayre and a team believed to be the Lincoln County Patriots. (Courtesy of Sayre School.)

The Lions of Lexington Christian School pose for a 1987–1988 team photograph. From left to right are (first row) David Miller, Matt Preston, Lynn Beach, Brad Beach, and Shane Jennings; (second row) Steve Rainwater, Robert Ray, Scott Ulery, John Moody, and Sean Alcorn. The team finished in third place in the KCAA State Tournament. (Courtesy of Lexington Christian Academy.)

Bryan Station's Craig Brooks blocks a shot attempt from an unidentified Tates Creek player in the semifinal of the 1988 43rd District Tournament. The Bryan Station Defenders went on to win the game 60-42 and become district champions with a 63-61 victory over Henry Clay. (Courtesy of Bryan Station High School.)

Lexington Christian School's Matt Preston puts up a shot during the 1988–1989 season. This would be the last season for the Lions playing within the KCAA, as the following year, they would become Lexington Christian Academy and join the Kentucky High School Athletic Association. (Courtesy of Lexington Christian Academy.)

During the 1988–1989 season, Bryan Station and Henry Clay players battle for a loose ball in one of the three games between the schools. Bryan Station won the first meeting 67-65 but would lose the next two by the scores of 57-68 and 65-67. (Courtesy of Bryan Station High School.)

6

THE 1990S

The Lexington Christian Academy fields its first team under the new school name and playing within the Kentucky High School Athletic Association. Under the leadership of head coach Tommy Starns, it seems that the Eagles' first varsity team consisted of just eight players. (Courtesy of Lexington Christian Academy.)

Bryan Station's Wesley Johnson goes to ground in an attempt to gain possession in a game against Fairdale in his senior season of 1989–1990. The Bryan Station Defenders lost this encounter by a score of 68-61. (Courtesy of Bryan Station High School.)

The first squad to represent Paul Laurence Dunbar High School poses for a photograph prior to the 1990–1991 season. The team would conclude the season with a 13-11 record. Pictured from left to right are (first row) Steven Estepp, Shane Robertson, Tommy Kiger, Alonzo Alcorn, Jamie Haydon, Isaac Sanders, Nicky Nickles, Jeff DeBelvue, Tim Stewart, Thaddeus Byrd, Seth Berry, and Juan Jackson; (second row) head coach Frank Watson, assistant coach Mike Fannin, Shad Wilson, Kevin Wilson, Jason West, Sean Edwards, Dennis Allen, Lumi Travis, Troy Black, coach Carl Jones, and coach Kenny Southworth; (third row) Stevie Mays, Eric Trigg, Cameron Mills, David Tavis, Darnell Burton, William Mayfield, Brad Horn, Jarrod Martin, Tony Olinger, and Brandon Lattae. (Courtesy of Paul Laurence Dunbar High School.)

With two defenders between himself and the basket, Sayre's Tyler Nahra attempts a hook shot in this game from the Spartans' 1990–1991 season. (Courtesy of Sayre School.)

Paul Laurence Dunbar's Lumie Travis rises toward the basket in this Bluegrass Invitational game against Lexington Catholic. The Knights would go on to defeat Dunbar 61-57 in this matchup from the 1990–1991 season. (Courtesy of Paul Laurence Dunbar High School.)

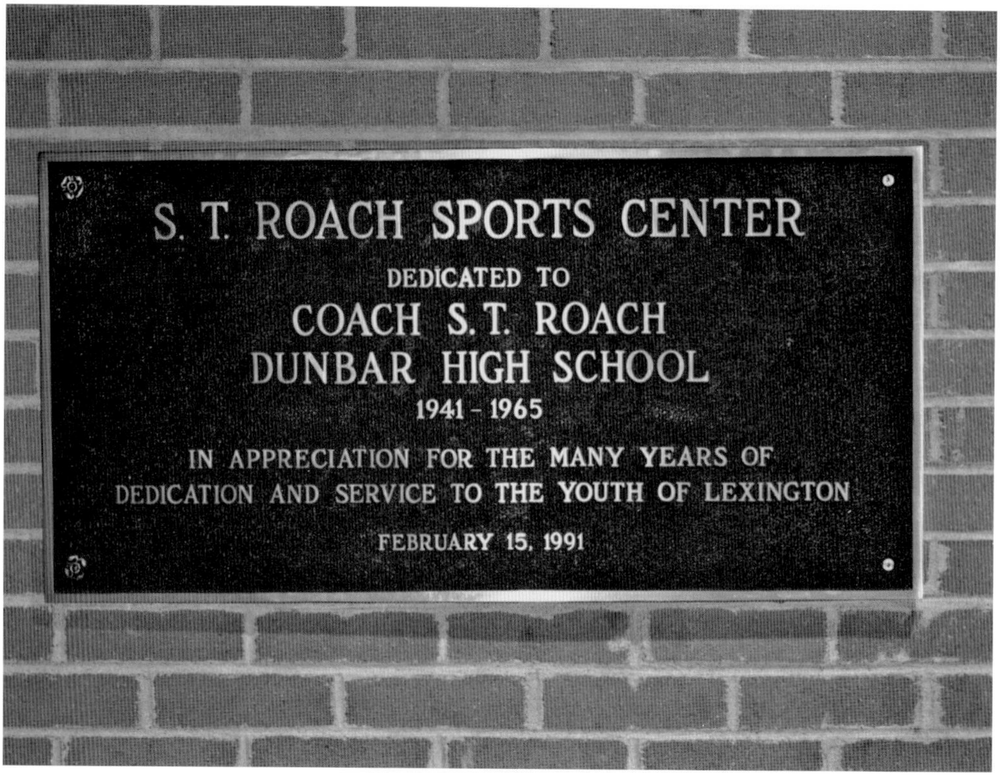

Paul Laurence Dunbar High School named its gymnasium the S. T. Roach Sports Center on February 15, 1991, in appreciation of S. T. Roach, the esteemed coach of the original Dunbar Bearcats basketball team. (Photograph by Kismet Photography, courtesy of author's personal collection.)

The Tates Creek players stand disconsolate after their state championship loss to Fairdale by a score of 67-63 at Rupp Arena in 1991. (Courtesy of Tates Creek High School.)

Paul Laurence Dunbar's Tim Stewart (12) guards a Henry Clay opponent in a game from the 1991–1992 season. The two teams played each other twice, sharing the honors, with Henry Clay victorious in the first game 84-83 and Dunbar taking the second game 83-74. (Courtesy of Paul Laurence Dunbar High School.)

The Sayre Spartans of the 1991–1992 season ready themselves for the campaign. Pictured from left to right are (first row) Whit Moloney, Ryan Adkins, Brentley Jones, Joe Cowles, Jamie Durham, Brian Graves, and Barry Mitchell; (second row) coach Jamie Lamonica, coach Jay Parsons, Geoff Dunn, Tyler Nahra, Ian Abbott, Jim Mason, Jason Brown, and coach Donny Weir; (third row) Joey Palumbo, Steve Johnson, Matt Mason, Jason Conway, Jimmy Hatfield, Jesse McGreevy, and Johnny Palumbo. (Courtesy of Sayre School.)

A crowd gathers under the basket during a game between Bryan Station and Casey County during the 1992–1993 season. Bryan Station went on to win this game by a score of 90-60. (Courtesy of Bryan Station High School.)

The 1992–1993 Paul Laurence Dunbar team have a squad photograph taken. Pictured from left to right are (first row) Terrence Huguely, Lumie Travis, Jeff Baker, Alonzo Alcorn, Tim Stewart, Troy Black, Derrick Cummins, and Greg Jones; (second row) coach Mike Fannin, coach Bob Jones, Billy Mayfield, Darnell Burton, Cameron Mills, David Tavis, Brad Horn, Daniel Melcher, Travis Byars, and coach Frank Watson. (Courtesy of Paul Laurence Dunbar High School.)

The 1992–1993 Tates Creek squad poses for a team photograph. The size of the squad shows how far the sport of basketball had come since the halcyon days of the early teams. Portrayed in this photograph are the varsity, junior varsity, and freshman squads, along with their coaches and the support staff needed to run such a program. (Courtesy of Tates Creek High School.)

The Paul Laurence Dunbar faithful show their support for the television cameras as the Bulldogs perform in the 1993 11th Region Tournament. (Courtesy of Paul Laurence Dunbar High School.)

Bryan Station senior Barry Bowman throws down a dunk during the 1992–1993 season. The Defenders would become 43rd District champions but would go on to lose in the 11th Region final. Both games were played against Paul Laurence Dunbar. (Courtesy of Bryan Station High School.)

Greg Jones drives to the basket for Paul Laurence Dunbar in a game against Lafayette during the 1993–1994 season. Dunbar defeated Lafayette on all three occasions they met that year by the scores of 70-48, 63-57, and 78-60. (Courtesy of Paul Laurence Dunbar High School.)

Paul Laurence Dunbar's Cameron Mills poses for an individual photo shoot during the 1993–1994 season. Mills would go on to play for the University of Kentucky team that won the NCAA Championship in both 1996 and 1998. (Courtesy of Paul Laurence Dunbar High School.)

Cameron Mills cuts down the net for Paul Laurence Dunbar after the 74-73 11th Region Championship victory over Lexington Catholic in 1994. (Courtesy of Paul Laurence Dunbar High School.)

The Paul Laurence Dunbar cheerleaders can't hold back their tears as their Bulldogs lost the 1994 State Championship to Fairdale, 59-56. (Courtesy of Paul Laurence Dunbar High School.)

Cameron Mills heads toward the basket during Paul Laurence Dunbar's 1994 11th Region Championship game against Lexington Catholic. (Courtesy of Paul Laurence Dunbar High School.)

Paul Laurence Dunbar's Lumie Travis seems to have supernatural control over the basketball during the 1994 State Championship game against Fairdale. (Courtesy of Paul Laurence Dunbar High School.)

Paul Laurence Dunbar's Terence Hugueley rises high to get a jump shot off against Tates Creek in a game from the 1994–1995 season. The Bulldogs played the Tates Creek Commodores three times that season, losing 60-59 and 60-57 before winning the third encounter 67-66. (Courtesy of Paul Laurence Dunbar High School.)

Lexington Catholic's Derrick White pulls up for a jump shot in a game against Bryan Station during the 1995–1996 season. (Courtesy of Lexington Catholic High School.)

Henry Clay senior Cory Owsley scores a basket as he takes advantage of a fast-break opportunity in a game during the 1995–1996 campaign. (Courtesy of Henry Clay High School.)

The Lexington Christian Academy Eagles ready themselves for the 1996–1997 season by posing for a team photograph. From left to right are (first row) Steve Brown, O'Ryan McCray, Austin Ketron, Matt Jones, Stephen Turner, T. J. Wright, Aaron Hicks, Hunter Garner, and Eric Vasques; (second row) head coach David Cravens, coach ? Flora, Mike Miller, Matt Steely, Tyler Langley, Andrew Brown, Justin Scott, Seth Stanton, coach ? Tackett, and coach ? True. (Courtesy of Lexington Christian Academy.)

Henry Clay's Ronnie Carson (23) is fouled by a Bryan Station Defender in a game from the 1996–1997 season. The Defenders won both meetings that season by the scores of 68-44 and 83-43. (Courtesy of Henry Clay High School.)

Paul Laurence Dunbar senior Jo Jo Dunn puts a shot over the outstretched arms of Paintsville's J. R. Vanhoose during their 1997 Sweet Sixteen clash. Paintsville would progress in the tournament courtesy of a score of 87-67. (Courtesy of Paul Laurence Dunbar High School.)

Henry Clay's Brandon Everman (21) goes for a layup under pressure from a Lafayette defender in a game during the 1996–1997 season. The two schools met three times that season, with the Lafayette Generals taking the honors each time by the scores of 96-62, 90-67, and 69-57. (Courtesy of Henry Clay High School.)

Sayre's Brad Nahra attempts to break through the Montgomery County defense in a game played on December 5, 1997. Sayre won the game by a score of 72-44. (Courtesy of Sayre School.)

The 1997–1998 Paul Laurence Dunbar Bulldogs pose for a photograph. Pictured from left to right are (first row) David Watson, Rayshon Williams, Clark Tatum, Wes Rainey, Nick Runyon, Antoine Beatty, Eric Burton, and Eddie Smith; (second row) Ryan Sakee, Jason Slates, coach ? Watson, coach ? Woods, head coach Frank Watson, coach ? Jones, coach ? Wilson, and Jessica Dye; (third row) George Baker, Brian Hundley, Marshall Wassel, Matt Anderson, Scott Hundley, Matt Easter, Jimmy Kosieniak, and A. J. Ellis. (Courtesy of Paul Laurence Dunbar High School.)

Sayre's Grayson Vendegrift drives past the defense in a game against Lexington Catholic during the 1998–1999 season. The schools played each other three times that season, including a 43rd District clash, with the Lexington Catholic Knights taking the honors each time by scores of 95-52, 83-36, and 79-36. (Courtesy of Sayre School.)

The end of the 1997–1998 season saw Lexington Christian Academy graduate three seniors from its basketball team. They were (from left to right) David Sternberg, Stephen Turner, and Garret Mourn. (Courtesy of Lexington Christian Academy.)

Lexington Catholic's Lawrence Board pulls down an offensive rebound in a game against West Jessamine during the 1998–1999 season. The teams met three times that season, with the Lexington Catholic Knights emerging victorious in all three by the scores of 89-50, 71-59, and a 91-38 win in the district tournament. (Courtesy of Lexington Catholic High School.)

7

THE 2000S

The 1999–2000 Paul Laurence Dunbar squad consisted of, from left to right, (first row) Steve Greene, Brannon Dunn, David Watson, Rayshon Williams, Jerrico Goree, Kelley Williams, Spurgeon Mayes, and Chaz-Lee Clifford; (second row) Clark Tatum, coach Brian Davis, coach Deron Norman, coach Charles Thomas, coach Eddie Oakley, coach Jim Lankster, coach Mike Watson, coach Jerome Hoosier, and Allen Penn; (third row) Matt Ledbetter, Matt Williams, David Byars, Alexious Osumenya, Kenneth Fox, Roderick Lyvers, Clay Tate, and Waltclaire Flynn. (Courtesy of Paul Laurence Dunbar High School.)

Sayre's Joe Porter puts up a shot in the home game against Harrodsburg played on February 12, 2000. Sayre would fall to Harrodsburg in this game by a score of 70-56. (Courtesy of Sayre School.)

The Paul Laurence Dunbar team of 2000–2001 poses for a photograph. From left to right are (first row) Chaz-Lee Clifford, J. J. Johnson, Jamie Adams, Robert Wint, Marcus Conner, Mike Matthews, Steven Greene, A. J. Johnson, and Justin Frees; (second row) Jeremy Howard, coach Mike Watson, coach Deron Norman, Allen Penn, Dean Haggard, John Michael Boggs, Kenny Hale, head coach Ed Oakley, coach Jim Lankster, and coach Jerome Hoosier; (third row) Clay Tate, David Kovacic, David Byars, Justin Sok, Kenneth Fox, Rod Lyvers, Landry Buckner, Anthony Davis, and Kenny Bledsoe. (Courtesy of Paul Laurence Dunbar High School.)

The Henry Clay Blue Devils ready themselves for the 2001–2002 season. Pictured from left to right are (first row) assistant coach Jay Brodas, Noade Day, Brandon Coles, Lamont Campbell, Eric Clift, Branden Bowman, and assistant coach Mark Thompson; (second row) head coach Kirk Chiles, Bryan Turnage, Todd Kessinger, Clay List, John Patterson, Beau Sandage, Chase Mitchell, and assistant coach Daniel Brown. (Courtesy of Henry Clay High School.)

The Paul Laurence Dunbar Bulldogs pose for a photograph after winning the 2001 Berea Christmas Tournament. (Courtesy of Paul Laurence Dunbar High School.)

Blue Grass Baptist's Drew Hammonds starts a drive toward the basket in a 2001–2002 game. The Blue Grass Baptist School plays within the Kentucky Christian Athletics Association (KCAA). (Courtesy of Blue Grass Baptist School.)

The Bulldogs of Paul Laurence Dunbar pose for a 2002–2003 season photograph. Pictured from left to right are (first row) Mike Matthews, Dustin Fox, Jamie Adams, Justin Frees, and Marcus Conner; (second row) Kenny Hale, Sekoe White, Justin Sok, Landry Buckner, Jeff Sandberg, Jason Azubuike, and Bobby Vyverberg. (Courtesy of Paul Laurence Dunbar High School.)

John Patterson (50) blocks a Lafayette shot for his Henry Clay team in the 2003 district tournament final. Henry Clay won the game 60-53 and would eventually advance all the way to the semifinals of the Sweet Sixteen. (Courtesy of Henry Clay High School.)

Henry Clay's Aubrey White (30) is trailed by John Patterson (50) on a fast break in the 2003 state tournament first-round game against Iroquois. The Blue Devils would advance to face Warren Central thanks to an 81-80 victory in overtime. (Courtesy of Henry Clay High School.)

Bryan Turnage (33) of Henry Clay puts up a jump shot against Lafayette during the district tournament final. The Blue Devils would finish the season at Rupp Arena with a record of 28-5. (Courtesy of Henry Clay High School.)

Doug Arnold of Sayre attacks the West Jessamine defense in a game played on January 3, 2004, in Nicholasville. West Jessamine won the game 66-59. (Courtesy of Sayre School.)

Senior Lamont Campbell ends his high school career with Henry Clay on the floor of Rupp Arena after a 84-77 loss to Ballard in the semifinals of the 2003 Sweet Sixteen. (Courtesy of Henry Clay High School.)

Blue Grass Baptist's three graduating seniors of the 2005–2006 season were Tony Ashcraft (24), Larry Broughton (55), and Joseph Robinson (22). (Courtesy of Blue Grass Baptist School.)

The 2004–2005 version of the Paul Laurence Dunbar Bulldogs included, from left to right, (first row) Dion Johnson, Mike Jones, Anthony Jones, A. J. Hartsfield, Chris Watson, Andre Tunstill, Leonard Epps, Brian Hatton, and Jesse Moton; (second row) coach Mike Watson, coach Derrick Thomas, Dustin Fox, Brandon Sok, Chris Sandford, Sean Hager, coach Eddie Oakley, coach Robert Goodman, and coach Barry Mitchell. (Courtesy of Paul Laurence Dunbar High School.)

Tates Creek's John Watkins is the masked man attacking the basket in a game against Madison Central during the 2006–2007 season. Central went on to defeat Tates Creek by a score of 69-63. (Courtesy of Tates Creek High School.)

Trae Cunningham of Sayre protects the ball from the challenge of a Lexington Christian Academy defender during the 2006–2007 campaign. (Courtesy of Sayre School.)

University Heights' candidate for the 2008 Mr. Basketball award, Scottie Hopson, attempts to block an incoming shot from Mike Sparks of Tates Creek. The Tates Creek Commodores emerged victorious from this encounter with a 86-59 score. (Courtesy of Tates Creek High School.)

Lexington Catholic made it all the way to the Sweet Sixteen semifinals in 2008 before losing to eventual runners-up Holmes. This photograph shows action from the team's second-round game against Owensboro at Rupp Arena. The Knights won the game by a score of 54-47. (Photograph by Kismet Photography, from the author's personal collection.)

They Coached in Fayette County

Adolph Rupp Jr., son of the famed University of Kentucky coach Adolph Rupp Sr., coached with many local high school teams after he graduated from University High and the University of Kentucky, where he played for his father. Here he is pictured with assistant coach Harold Barnett (right) during a 43rd District Tournament game while head coach at Lafayette in 1965. (Courtesy of author's personal collection.)

Pictured here are Lafayette's head coach, Jock Sutherland, and his assistant, Don Harville, in am image taken from a program from the 1972–1973 season. The accompanying text states that Sutherland was named coach of the year in 1963 and 1966, was appointed coach for the annual Kentucky–Indiana games for 1973, and had a record of 347-119 at that point in his career. (Courtesy of author's personal collection.)

Coach John G. Heber of Lexington and Henry Clay ended his 23-year career with a record of 310-162 and coached his team to a state championship in 1924. In addition to boys' basketball, Heber also coached football, track, and the girls' basketball team. (Courtesy of Henry Clay High School.)

Tates Creek's head coach from 1971 to 1999 was Nolan Barger. A graduate of Transylvania University, Barger ended his career with a record of 540-260, was voted coach of the year in 1973, and led his Commodores to the state tournament final in 1991. (Courtesy of Tates Creek High School.)

Pictured here is storied Dunbar coach S. T. Roach. Sporting a 610-166 career record, Roach coached his Dunbar team to two state runner-up finishes after integration into the Kentucky High School Athletics Association. Paul Laurence Dunbar honored Roach by naming its gymnasium and the annual S. T. Roach Classic tournament after him. (Courtesy of Paul Laurence Dunbar High School.)

Gene Huff coached the University High Purples from 1956 to 1965, the year that the school closed. Among the players Huff coached was Adolph Rupp Jr. Rupp's father would frequently discuss basketball and tactics with Huff in the halls of the school and Memorial Coliseum. (Courtesy of Gene Huff.)

Kirk Chiles had a coaching career that spanned 26 years and five different schools, including Henry Clay. Chiles ended his career with a record of 516-272. (Courtesy of Henry Clay High School.)

Louis Stout is pictured below being interviewed by a local television station while a coach at Tates Creek in 1972. Stout is probably better known as the commissioner of the Kentucky High School Athletic Association, a position he held for eight years. Stout was the first African American to head a state athletic association office. (Courtesy of Tates Creek High School.)

Paul Laurence Dunbar head coach Frank Watson took his team to the state championship final in consecutive years in 1993 and 1994, both times finishing the season as runners-up. (Courtesy of Paul Laurence Dunbar High School.)

Lexington Catholic head coach Tommy Starns is pictured talking to his team during a time-out in the 1969–1970 season. Starns took his Knights to the Sweet Sixteen in 1966, 1977, and 1985. (Courtesy of Lexington Catholic High School.)